Belongings

for Cathal Ó Searcaigh

Joan Newmann ¦ Kate Newmann

BELONGINGS

ARLEN
HOUSE

Published in 2007 by
ARLEN HOUSE
an imprint of Arlen Publications Ltd
PO Box 222
Galway, Ireland
Phone/Fax: 353 86 8207617
Email: arlenhouse@gmail.com

Distributed in North America by
SYRACUSE UNIVERSITY PRESS
621 Skytop Road, Suite 110
Syracuse, NY 13244–5290
Phone: 315–443–5534/Fax: 315–443–5545
Email: supress@syr.edu

ISBN 978–1–903631–63–8, paperback

The cover painting 'La mujer del huevo' by Alfonso
Monreal is used with the kind permission of the artist

Typesetting ¦ Arlen House
Printing ¦ Betaprint

Contents

ACKNOWLEDGEMENTS

Some of these poems have been previously published
in: *Poetry Ireland Review*, *HU*; *Thin Ice* (Abbey Press,
Newry); *Edgeworth Papers*; *Poetry* (Chicago); *The Living
Stream* (A Festschrift for Theo Dorgan); *Cyphers*; *Signals
Anthology* (Abbey Press, Newry); *Verse* (Fyfe); *The Crazy
Knot* (Bangor Printworks); *The Newfoundland Quarterly*;
Quadrant (Australia); *Atlanta Review*; *Brass on Bronze*
(Errigal Writers' Anthology); *Writing Women*
(Newcastle-upon-Tyne); *Voices from the Rock Anthology*
(Newfoundland); *The White Page* (Salmon Press); *Word
of Mouth Anthology* (Blackstaff Press); *80 MPH* (A
Festschrift for Leland Bardwell); *Fortnight*; *The SHOp*;
Orbis; *Listowel Anthology 2003*; *Decanto*; *Breaking the Skin*
(Black Mountain Press); *Envoi*; *Poetry Now*; *Scealta Staire
Chill Chartha*; *De Brakke Hund* (Belgium); *Carapace*
(South Africa).

Some of these poems have been translated into
Russian and Spanish.

JOAN NEWMANN

APPLE

Which apple?
Lord Lambourne? Worcester Permain?
Woody bitter crab?
Apples of childhood without names –
yellow-skinned, vaguely musty,
a neighbour's gift, windfalls,
brown splotch of decay?

Apples on the Old Rectory trees.
Sitting, summer legs sore on branches,
eating at autumn with the reach of a hand,
throwing sucked cores down through golden air
for fussy russet hens to run at.

Loughgall and Richhill Bramleys,
peeled in a white delft bowl, turning tan.
Shush of knife on apple flesh.
Stolen slices, sugar crystals moist
on moisture – tart, tart.

The apple, green as green Granny Smith
Eileen McKenna and I bought
in Cissie White's for ninepence.
She walking me part of the way home,
passing it for jaw-sized bites,
slobbering juices on our chins.
Perfection. Past our bedtime and it still light.

Adam, I did not give you the apple.
Had you not taken, bitten strong,
colour for the hungry soul,
essence skiting from your teeth,
we never would have known.

RED SHOES 1944

It was for the Christmas cake
into the oily lamp light
from the Dundalk bus;
the shuffle of stiff paper,
smuggled sugar and butter and currants
and cherries and almonds
and muscats, muscats, muscats
Don't eat them all they're for the baking.

And Carrie – the smallest pair of red shoes,
her anxious eyes – *Do they fit her?*
She who knew my feet by bone by bone by bone.
All their shadows reach down,
fumble the beady black buttons.
Red real leather below my night-dress.
I am told to *Walk in them. Walk them in.*

The stiffness, heavy on warm skin
sound like a visitor on the stone floor.
I am nothing – all shoes.
They're not hurting you? Carrie talking
into my eyes. I shake my head.

O I am forever shod in redness.

PASSING THE SIGN TO DRUMBANAGHER
AND THE DROMANTINE MISSIONS

It was the day we went on the bus fifty-two years ago
and Muriel told me about the woman
who had been stung by a bee
and the bee was still a lump above her eye
and the other woman, who had a bee in her mouth
and it stung her throat and tongue
and it all swelled up
and she died.

We were outside the house of the woman
with the bee in her head, on the hottest day,
grass seeds and flies and the dryness of the grass.

If it was the woman with the bee in her forehead,
its anger in her brain,
we wanted to see.

And it was miles to the other house
and we weren't allowed to do anything.
Kenny was uneasy and we didn't
get anything to eat.
Muriel's aunt didn't want us in the whitewashed yard,
her eyes tight as suspicion.

Kenny ran past us and past us
in his cut-down trousers,
hitting at us without touching,
his mother's voice like scutch grass
over all we did.

The Dromantine Missionaries in Africa –
we thought of trying to find them
but knew they wouldn't want us either.

FEDERATION BISCUITS

Hilary Magennis was the chemist's daughter,
all Viyella with smocking and white piqué collars;
a pale gold girl who had for break
pastel marshmallow of Federation Biscuits –
marshmallow, like the viyella in pinks,
soft yellows, mauves.

Get some Federation Biscuits, I wheedled.
No, they're too dear, the closure.
I owe Hilary Magennis a Federation Biscuit,
the magic charm to bring them,
sugar glinting.

I opened my greaseproof paper lunch.
My Federations were flat and handled.
Hilary, concealing her dismay said,
Thank you. Really. No.

MR AND MRS MARSHALL'S DINNERS

If you were bright in a desk
you could be chosen

to walk in the air hundreds of yards
to the house with the evergreens,

the house as sedate and chill
as the teachers themselves.

You would knock on the back door
knowing you were on hallowed ground

and Miss Boomer, Mrs Marshall's sister
would look down at you

despising and mildly amused.
She would reach you the big wicker basket

its handle worn by eager hands.
This was Mr and Mrs Marshall's dinner.

It was heavy – you could not drop it –
nor could you put it down.

What it taught you: your weight
pitted against its weight –

balance of worry and spill –
time between here and the bell –

the hot meat smell as the plates shifted –
fear of falling and the clipped thanks.

THIN ICE
for Audrey

I cry to go with my brother.
They leave me far behind,
wait at the gate of Henderson's field.
I am to walk across the pond,
a child Jesus on chill glass.
Arms cannot touch –
the high lift of my feet –
skreak and craze – craze
all silver and faraway green.
No breathing nerves tightrope,
ice warning of its substance
skreak and craze – hard shoes
laid down, footless.
Ice-girl, I see the weedy water
glazed as through a cataract
my own eyes cast down frozen.

SATURDAY EVENING POST

It was Annie Greenlee and her pale sister Grace,
their white hair curled static, neat pastel coats:
they brought Scotland into Mullavilly,
they brought the *Saturday Evening Post*.

By reading out loud, long before school untaught me,
and with an ear to the women – *Mrs Kettle says*
her man won't leave her alone and
They say it was the size of a grapefruit –
I went with the Broons, Ma astray in the heed;
with Horace and his sister Maggie
after the boys, and Daphne always for disappointment
nursing the bairn, and Pa taking us all
to the But and Ben
and you could have rung the sheets out.

There'd be tea and currant loaf,
good cups and half a flat Victoria sandwich cake
because it went further, white iced.
And Charlie Grant said he couldn't
get the lid on the coffin.

The tea cups waiting for hot water
as if their time was up and the china cabinet
might lock them out forever.
And did you see the hat he was wearing,
home from America, buying everybody
in the pub and him reared in a drawer.

I was there, better off than Oor Wullie,
on his upturned bucket wi nae money,
nae sweeties and naithin to dae.

ROUNDERS
in memory of William Turner

The field in new hay;
cut hedges for the burning;
front grass, warm smell of dusk dew.
And my uncle running to bowl.
My aunts in short-sleeved dresses, laughing like girls.
Even my mother, saying we should go in,
caught and held the ball my brother hit,
coming at her like an orb of solid darkness;
a child-skill remembered somewhere between knuckle
    and fist.
Flowers taking in their petals; heavy honeyed
night-scent of turkcap lilies;
whisper of mist on sycamore leaves
and my uncle running out of the dimness,
night cry of roosting birds,
swinging his arms in a fierceness.
From his hand the gentle
fall of ball upon my astounded, waiting bat.

SHERBET DIP

A long way to the prefabs on the Hamilton's Bawn
    Road,
it was Lettie and the twins,
new in the milky paleness of their skin,
in their twin pram like a caravel
bound for the New World, crew invisible,
their mother sewing so hard at the machine,
its stutter and rapid-fire in the bare room,
and the babies sleeping below deck
and the needle never went through Lettie's finger.

I sat on the cold grey step,
a bag of sherbet like gold dust
lasting as long as the indifferent afternoon,
rocketing behind my nostrils like new lemonade.
Being alone and passing beyond their imagination.

The Gramophone

And Muriel said
they had brand new needles
and you picked one out, thick-end,
from the tin box with the nightingale,
screw fixing it until it could sing.

We held the records – slabs of sound –
as carefully as Moses had carried
down from the mountain
the tablets of stone.

We sat on the stone floor
and Muriel said she had to do it
because it was theirs.
Cranking up the machine
the craning head
met the groove
and an accordion,
jigs and hornpipes
and John McCormack and
someone playing a fiddle
and John McCormack,
his voice drowning into a breathless gasp.

And once, I was allowed
to grasp that handle and with all my will
bring John McCormack back through
our giggles and splutterings to a great crescendo.
Did Moses ever feel such reverence
on a Sunday afternoon?

HARMONIUM
for Helen

The private dark of the room,
floorboards marked by years of shoe soles,
big iron bedstead, tarnished brass knobs.
Coats; flimsy draping things;
dark blankets; goose down;
feather in ticking, cuddling you,
you drowning in it to smothering.
The oil lamp, and there it was,
the harmonium – Dorrie raising the dust
and *What a friend we have in Jesus* –
the pedals screaking and gasping,
the lamp's glow frantic to decipher the notes
on the onion-skin paper.
Huge ghosts of ourselves cavorting walls
and ceiling. Dorrie singing
for all of Mullahead to hear,
Muriel bellowing every word,
for they were Methodists.
And *What a friend we have in Jesus.*
It was so easy to believe it all.

Lily and Kathleen

KATHLEEN SHOUTING AT THE NEIGHBOURS

She looked into the meadow over the scrawny hedge,
and in the hush of evening light on the ragwort
Sheila was milking the brown cow –
the one that could move away
and spill the milk.

Your child's a bastard.
Sheila's head on the cow's familiar belly.
Hey – your child is a bastard,
and maybe more. But she hung
lead weights on the threads of truth
we knew about each other
until we could not lift our eyes.

KATHLEEN AND THE NEWRY BUS

We never saw Kathleen
until she started to walk the roads.
She jumped out of the ditch
in front of the last bus to Newry,
the driver staring at her,
her eyebrows coarse and grey,
under the black beret
eyes like winter skies,
cream belted raincoat, bare legs.

*On the road at that time
of night*, they said. *They are taking her
to St. Luke's.* When she returned
shocked to her core, she never left her room
and forgot that she hadn't meant the bus to stop.

LILY AT THE PUMP

She had a goitre.
It must be bigger than a grapefruit, they said.
A goitre's better on the outside, they said,
it doesn't kill you.
You would think she would cover it
with a scarf or something.

Lily came for water to our pump
and I stared through the railings
and she would smile,
all nonsense words
breaking down to laughing.
And sometimes I thought I saw
the goitre swing – and would
it burst while I was looking?

LILY AND THE COMPETITIONS

When was the Battle of Waterloo?
Give an example of a palindrome.
Able was I ere I saw Elba.
Who shot Abraham Lincoln?
What is the date of the summer solstice?

Lily knew it all, and I would post the answers
and twice we won – the prizes
a knitting-needle bag for very short needles
and a red and yellow plastic toadstool
with a screw-off top. Lily laughed and laughed.

Lily's Goitre and my Mumps and the Oranges

I swelled on my left side,
the same as Lily's goitre
and in the mirror I had no neck, no chin.

I was full of food desires
from reading *Christmas Carol*
and there was not a thing in our grey kitchen that
looked like food. Lily stood at the pump,
in her hand a brown paper bag.
All the oranges bigger than appetite
fell on the patchwork quilt.
They smelt like imagination
and their pith and peels tasted like love.

THE SMOKY LAMP IN THE DIRTY WINDOW
IN THE MIDDLE OF THE NIGHT

It was there in Kathleen's room,
that small yellow defiance
in the black that suffocated
Ballyknock at night,
when the feet of the stranger
stopped your breathing.

They keep the fire lit all night, they said,
and they read all night, they said,
and they never go to bed, they said,
and they read all night, they said.

Able was I ere I saw Elba.
They read all night.

The Cats, the Breadman, the Milkman and the Turfman

Lily stopped going to Tandragee
for oranges – for oranges.

*And you should see the armfuls of bread she gets from the
    breadman –*
every day, they said.
And the milkman leaves six pints, they said, *every day.*
And the turfman – well you should see what he carries in –
cabbages, and the potatoes.

And the bread and milk fed
the amazing breeding cats.
They are everywhere, they said.
Lily ate cabbage and potatoes and read all night.

The Council Fixes Lily and Kathleen's House

A new bathroom.
But they wanted their lavatory outside,
and there was so much coal,
electricity was meaningless.
And there was coal everywhere.
The Council built a new chimney
which belched smoke back into the room.

You should see their faces
and the inside of the place
is like looking into hell, they said.

It was then that Lily locked her gate.

KATHLEEN IN HOSPITAL

She can't stop washing her hands, they said.
They have to tie her in the bed,
or else she is up washing and washing
her hands.

THE ENDING OF KATHLEEN

Oh no – Lily's on her own.
Kathleen's dead, they said.

I Show Lily my Baby

Don't be going down there, they said.
She won't hear you. She won't come out,
they said, *and your tea is ready*
and it's far too cold to take the child out.

I carry the baby
against the Sunday chill
and call Lily's name, Lily's name,
Lily's name at the locked gate
and the cats
in the pine tree scrabble and hide
and Lily comes to the door,
walks up the steep hill of her path,
her eyes wonderful grey and startling.

And she looks at the infant in my arms
Ah, ah, she says, *would you look at that,*
Ah, ah – and her goitre is ingrained with dirt and her
  hair
is a witchery grey and
her hands do not reach out for us.
Would you look at that,
as though I had done something
very clever or very stupid.

LILY AND THE STONE THROWERS

The children walk from the town to mock,
throw stones that blatter off the front door.
They want Lily and her goitre
to come out and shout
and nobody stops them – the bastards.

MEASLED

Lily sits close to the flame.
Have you seen her legs, they say,
measled by the fire.
God Bless us, you should see them –
purple red, they say.

LILY IN THE HOSPITAL

The hospital, its filth well hidden
by chemicals lying heavy on all the surfaces.

The nurses helping her,
stooped, back to her bed.
She is white and the flowers
on her wynciette nightdress
are faded.

Do you remember this lady? they say.
She looks me in the eye,
her head hanging.

Able was I ere I saw Elba.

How did they scrub clean
the goitre with a soapy cloth?
Were they not afraid?

The Last Time I See Lily

Far better in the hospital, they said.
Who will they get to destroy the cats, they said.
They say if you had only seen the house, they said,
it would have taken the light
from your eyes, they said.

Lily was bent double at the last, they said.
Back bent bearing Ballyknock bigotry
they never said.

SOLVING THE MYSTERY OF THE PLASTIC TOADSTOOL

I saw a woman
with a plastic toadstool.
The inside held a bulb
and you stretched the hole
in the heel of your sock
over the spotty cap
and the light meant
you could darn in the dark.

Able was I ere I saw Elba.

THE RED STAR TO OMEATH

It was a Sunday and Jerretspass,
Poyntzpass, Drumbanagher, Newry,
Narrow Water to Warrenpoint, the Mournes.

And the bus load of us,
our feet crunching the sea-stones,
crushing onto the Red Star
low in the water, its old engine
aching. Low in the water
your hand able to lift Carlingford Lough.

And spread up the jetty,
stalls quivering with cockles and mussels,
the fairy hair of candy-floss,
pink peppermint rock: your spittle
could melt *From Omeath*.

And the jaunting car, its horse
drawing us, our feet eye-level
to the walkers going to Calvary.

And the pub, the black smell of stout, the noise;
the women insisting on the hotel.
Hot whiskey – and there'd be more than two
lemonades.

Time to breathe it all into the mildest air;
salt, seaweed, sin.
It was only a few who cared if the boat left us here.

Children dazed by the length and breadth
of the yellow-sweet day;
the boat couping and jittering.

The women bleating *Oh … Oh … Oh*

Customs Officers could search you in their hut,
take away the sugar
you'd tried to hide inside your vest.
It must still have been the war.

Tea and tea in The Singing Kettle.
To thin serious days
the bus home – where?

THE FOSBURY FLOP

No. It was the Western Roll.
Miss McCormack teaching us to jump.
Mystery of airborne feet,
school bells singing, bar notching skyward.
And it was only me, and they
could not believe my body buoyant
with secrecy of flight.

With rope and posts at home,
it could be higher than trees.
I wanted them to envy.
O, I was sure as heron, astounding as swan.
Why did ostrich inhabit me?
Who clipped my wings – the sin of pride?
The Angels did not want me on their side.

Unwanted Hair

You said, lying in illicit ferns and moss,
Do you have hair under your armpits?
An ugliness scuttled over the cold stones
into my mouth. In thirteen years
of living we did not say
Do you have hair under your armpits?
Evening galloping into night,
I have to be home, I breathe,
I haven't a tail light on my bike.

If you have hair under your armpits,
you said, *you know what that means.*

PIANO
for Anna Cooper

O I can wash my Daddy's shirt,
O I can wash it clean,
O I can wash my Daddy's shirt
And hang it on the line.

Over-strung, its big teak body was mine.
Second-hand hymn book with real music,
monthly payments their own shameful harsh note.
Scales, arpeggios, playing by ear
which was supposed to be bad.

By the moon's magic
miracle of music made in us
... young Eileen was spinning ...
Merrily, cheerily, round goes the wheel now ...
crochet of sycamore leaves
trembling on the front room blind.

Step by Step to the Classics, book three:
Mozart's *Andante* – piano relieved
at last to sound like a piano.
Minuet in G – right hand poised
to take the dance from the left.

Years of silence in the damp room,
its fire kept for Christmas and death.
Piano's mouth firm shut
revealing a grimace of ivory
for *Rakes of Mallow* or *Blue Danube*
in a waiting Sunday on lazy whim.

A dark shed, rhythm of rain on the corrugated roof.
Drip, drip, your gums are swollen.
A child has written CDEFGAB on your yellow keys
with ballpoint pen. I bring piano
to block with untunedness, my hall.

How can I watch them carry piano – highly-strung,
heavy with years – for callous boys
to batter, not knowing each chord
tells of loud, ebullient laughter,
of fallings-out, sulky silence, anger.
Of misery, tears leaked sorrowfully
in the gulping dark.

PPPPPiano Piano Piano
PPPPPiano Piano …

WHIN BUSH
for Colin Middleton

Left forever telling it – your painting
I could not afford to have my eyes on.

A whin bush in the Mournes – glory of gold,
a burning bush,
growl of purple mountain rising at its back.

We'd stand pulling guarded flowers
to dye our eggs for Easter,
hope the few would be enough,
smelling like custard, like honey,
prickles spearing even vests
to taunt our winter skin.

Plump of water – flowers drowned, pellucid,
liquid colour of piss circled in aluminium.

Rolling ourselves, felled logs, down Cullin's hill,
'til it was time, 'til it was time for
eggs bouncing in pocks and ruts
hard-boiled yolk exploding yellow,
shells in cow dung. We'd eat the strange,
white lemonade fizzling with specialness,
bringing an oddness to lie upon the tongue,
a sacrament of bread and egg and bun.

Zero Mile Post

I am taken with Emma McMahon,
five foot eleven at the age of twelve,
she dreamed she knit a cardigan with sleeves the
length of Corbett's shop.

I – blood poisoning binding me to grey days –
am taken with Emma McMahon and her cigarettes
to Tandragee Picture House, old plush and lavatories.
Debbie Reynolds, small and clean and healthy
in *Tammy, Tammy, Tammy's in Love.*
I, like the chosen child from the Sierra Madre
kept in the dark until eyes are magic,
colours sink in the celluloid of me.

I am back in the land before the doctor said.
I am not supposed to be of the night,
chill in my hair, road under me.
They hold my damp hands. I walk
like a stilted sea-bird, its gawky feet.
We have missed the last train to San Fernando.

DEATH FEEDS ME
for Reesie

I am pressing the gnarl of sycamore bark
with scalp and skull.

It can't be the photograph,
me hanging on my uncle's shoulder
in a thick-washed jumper.
My mother backed against the snowcem
of the angular wall. My aunts
pausing on a journey elsewhere.
We are shrunk, grey, lens looking down on us
from beyond the grass bank, the pump,

because the men are walking
behind my mother's dead body.
Time is the day of the funeral.
We are left under the July sycamore
our eyes awater.
The house having coffined us
is letting it out
like an unreliable friend;
lavender essence – tea – roasting beef –
jazzle of china cup on china saucer.
In our ears the keen drop
of dark wet earth.

RUBY AND FRANK

Ruby and Frank, after my mother died,
took me on my bike to Mullahead.
Beside the Cusher River in the cattle hoof-marked
ground, we ate strawberries.
Frank kissed Ruby and in the heat of midday
we ate strawberries and lay on our backs,
the two of them – the one of me,
I, finding a place next to them.
Round by Moyallon and Gilford
singing without brakes downhill.
Tandragee, back to the wind – I don't remember
    Tandragee,
its castle, pink on sunset stone.
I don't remember ever coming home.

Free-Ranging Geese

in memory of James Simmons

The wild geese have come back,
unimagined whites in the flat winter fields,
carried here by the full sails
of their own wings.

The goose at Christmas –
large bones, little meat,
turned on its back,
cooked amber, amber,
a sauce of juniper berries
and port wine like brash in the mouth,
the flesh a forbidden knowledge.

Stand with each other, walk with each other,
your big whiteness like damask
on a green baize table.

You care not that our small eyes
intrude with impotence.
We can neither save nor foretell you.
You are too breast, too beak,
too faltering feet, for holiness.

THE ICEMAN COMETH
in memory of John Baird

ten women offered themselves as receptacles for the iceman's
five-thousand-year-old sperm

His copper axe with elbow shafting, birch tar, hafted
   in yew,
his pride – even the flaw, the shrink hole
tidied to obscurity; annoyance that time took him
before the axe-blade was re-ground.
A bow stave, fashioned for survival,
almost finished, placed with grace in his back pannier:
a man almost ready for the longest journey,
the cold coming. Dried tough ibex meat
eroding his teeth – *many more treks like this …*
he sucks in his cheeks and laughs,
the frontal gap dark and mocking.

Two birch-bark containers, one for carrying live
   embers;
small flint dagger, its cutting edges, broken tip, handle
   of ash
gloved in an exquisite plaited scabbard
his mother had made in the waiting,
a tool to sharpen it. A belt pouch
holding the scraper, bone awl, drilling tool, a piece of
   tinder,
a broken blade which caught and held the light.
Tinder fungus, pyrites to flare the dark,
melt snow to swallowing warmth.
Cosseted in leaves and grass
embers sometimes do not outlast the howl of night.
Twists of fur, a single whitish marble bead
around his wrist, threaded on leather,
two pieces of pierced birch fungus to repel the

sickness.
A single sloe to suck, bitten into wakefulness.
Sleep in the freezing place is death.

A net to tangle birds, quiver, arrow shafts.
He had already left, his spirit gone ahead,
fitting his fur cap, his poncho, a loin cloth, his
    leggings,
covering tattoos on ankle, foot, calf, knees and spine,
acupuncture points for his rheumatism.
His eyes encased in memory paths, ice floes.
He stuffs the netting of his leather shoes with grass for
    insulation
knowing that if your feet are cold, all of you is cold,
    cold.
That a rib break rants against the frost
and frostbite is the numbing enemy.

A plaited grass cloak, long-fringed, he left
in the grey dead light of chill morning,
would not prophesy a time for his return,
coming back impatient to bundle cord, stag antler and
    sinew,
guided in a knowledge of his need
by five hundred and fifty-two moons.

With his left arm stiff across his throat,
the hand helpless, hanging like the head
of a dead heron,
he was found, five thousand three hundred years
    older,
face-down on a rock in the ice of the Otztaler Alps,
and my son, he is your father.

MARY AND THE SPIKENARD

I spent the money my brother Lazarus willed to me
to buy a cask of spikenard
from the lofty regions of the Himalay –
unguent smelling strange of snow
of altitude, its small herbaceous root
pounded with pestle, trapped in lanolin,
clinging for life, a dizzy valerian.

Great heats these days make melt.
It has taken in where it is hidden
sweet dryness of fig leaves.

It is for the feet, where thorn has suppurated,
dull stone grazed, sandals chaffed.

I paid the price.
Let me not fear my brother's rage,
Martha's clenched perpetual anger.

Its name, *Nardostachys jatamans* – liquor on my lips.
Nardostachys jatamans – we salve the greatest hurt.

His breath on my hair on His perfumed feet.

Bonavista

MINNIE'S GOAT

I don't remember a word she spoke
but her forehead against the breathing side
of her Nubian goat
and the zip zip of the milk
into a tin can 'til it drowned
in the taste of its own froth
and the slow crooning fragments of care,
encouragement,
infinitely tender.

That you could say love in sounds
melted into my eyes.

DAVY'S LEG

Mauled in a threshing machine,
crushed in a quarry,
run over by a steamroller,
fallen on by a horse –
these things might have happened
to Davy's leg, held stiff
as metal, swung out
after his blackthorn stick.

Davy had a limp from The Accident,
    they said.
Did staring at it bring it home to me?

Minnie

Had a great gap between
her front teeth.
When you are eleven,
you are not kind.
Square cut hair, thick spectacles,
a gap between her legs
though you weren't supposed to say.

MINNIE'S CUSTARD

The way the food sits on the plate
in other people's houses,
coming to the table,
the dull knife and fork
fencing in that circle of delft,
its burden of bilious cabbage,
gum pink of the thin chop,
anaemic potatoes.
A gravy slick
making inedible islands of it.

And not to eat the food given,
not to eat the bread offered,
a deadly lack of faith.

Then the custard
solid in round clear glass dishes
and the anxious business of the hosts,
so few tinned pineapple chunks.

It was with dismay,
a thick spoonful in my mouth,
that I knew Minnie had put salt
in the custard.
We always do, was all she said.

AMERICAN DRESS

I know it was
all the colours of mauve and purple and cherry
Tandragee could not imagine
and it came out of the trunk from America
a piqué collar that detached
for washing and a black velvet ribbon
with ends to my waist
and it was too small for me
but what has that to do with vision.

I wore it staunchly,
moving past great-uncle Davy
in the tight back hall,
his lips lifted over his eye teeth,
the back of his hand moving over the American
    cotton,
over my nearly breasts.

THE FIRST DOUBLE-DECKER BUS

I had ever seen
and because they believed
that I should be through
the trees, nearer the sky,
they blundered up the steps
for me, the bag with boiled eggs
and buttered plain bread.
A flask because you didn't
waste your money in cafés.

Maybe what I saw
lifted me high enough
to sense it all.

The Brown Bear

His dry snout: standing upright
in a cage no bigger than himself;
his thick dull coat,
small enduring eyes.

Look at the bear!
Do you see the bear?
It can't touch you.
It can't get out,
Davy said, Minnie laughing.

I was not afraid
of the brown bear,
its claws ripping me.
I was afraid of what I smelt.

MINNIE AND DAVY'S VISIT

Minnie wrote a letter
on blue close-lined paper
to say that they
were coming to visit us,
that neither of them were
getting any younger,
that she'd like to see
the county that was Davy's.

If we would say
what suited us,
the family.

The family
did not reply.

DAVY'S FUNERAL

A quiet affair
leaving Minnie and the big house
and the amazing
Nubian goat with turquoise eyes.

Though the family
felt that
Minnie felt that they
should have paid the undertaker.

THE STEPS

What is left
is a grey photograph
at the top of the stone steps.

Davy in his suit,
hiding his stick,
grinning like a man
not used to laughter.
Me in the ridiculous
American dress and white sandals,
standing apart
as if touching
would betray all he held
behind his long, even teeth,
his hot squirming tongue.

MINNIE DIES

We never heard when.
Had she left the glens
to marry him late
for the good pension
and the big grey house
with the flight of steps?

I, only, hope the goat
– that fawn creature
fearing no hurt,
its cream ears,
the desert and secrets
in the tilt
of its arrogant head,
its goat eyes –
died first.

CAVE HILL

Davy wanted me to walk
with him up the Cave Hill
in the light before dark
when we looked down
on the boats' lisping quiet
on the pond and the silent
waltz of the Floral Ballroom,
the deadness of the zoo.

We walked slowly and did not speak
and we were far.

At the long hill's head
we stared over its green side.
There was a man
in a black-watch kilt
lying on top of a woman
all bundled together.

We came back slow
the evening covering us
and never said a word.

A NIGHT WITH AGAPPI
for Ann McKay

Serenity of high white ceiling, neutrality of four white
   walls;
Agappi's house, slid down Mount Ida as far as it was
   able,
hunched with holding on, facing its own handful of
   earth.
Night stillness, all-wool blankets and camphor,
bird screeches, a barking of dogs,
scent of olive trees cooling after heat,
window hung with cotton crochet,
jugged dry grasses spilling their seed,
huge jars for oil, for olives, for clothes, for grain,
their presences guarding me.
Swallowing and breathing sounds and smells,
pulling them over my head,
tangible cling of herbs on top of raki on my tongue.
A door locked from without
to protect my sleeping. Agappi reflecting
warm morning sun stands among her growing things.
I bend to kiss her, lips on light,
a gift of half her basil bush
singing pungent in my hands.

DANCING WITH MANUEL
for Maria and Kevin

The Spanish waiter
in the Port-na-Blagh Hotel,
his hard sinewy thigh
on the thin black cloth of his trousers
on the sheen of my glazed cotton skirt.
We were music, we were our skins
moving, night sea in our veins.

He smelt of hotter sun,
warm bread in the morning
and it was love that had
no words between us
ending with the last half note.

I understood then, consummation by dance,
but never found another partner
like Manuel, the Spanish waiter
in the Port-na-Blagh Hotel.

I HAVE BEEN THINKING OF THOMAS
FOR YEARS NOW
Milan Kundera

In Portadown Station,
a name label in his lapel,
Thomas Brady c/o
Gleneyre Children's Home.

What shapes a mouth?
His was twisted.

He bought me a second-hand handbag
in the market – watched my eyes.
The stagger of old lipstick stains,
rouge, the fearful smell of lust.

I lied well.
It was beautiful.

Out of the dark
he flung his hardness into me
because I would not see
because I would not see

the gift of bag
held all he had –
the gift of bag
had bought me.

I have been thinking of Thomas
for forty-three years now.

RICE
for Bridget Anne Ryan

Seven women, shin deep in watery mud
on a sweltering Sunday. They do not rise,
their fingers pushing root to soil
like infant mouth to milk, desiring survival.
They plant in rows so straight
an invisible line of rope
must be connecting them,
so at the same second seven stooped saris
move a step backwards under the threat
of the upright overseer and the indifference
of a white egret staring into green.

On my dinner plate, seven rice grains.
I slide them with a stern finger
onto my speechless tongue.

LABOUR

A Hindu woman
applying metal polish
to the brass handles
on the swing doors
of the Mandovi Hotel
with the skin
of her own hands.

CARRAGEEN MOUSSE AND THE BOY FROM NEPAL
for Prem

It sits on the plate like a white breast
on a lying woman.
Moss boiled in milk, a taste as seaward
as rock and sand, the dark grit
of where it has been.

His tongue expects rich buffalo milk
taken into the mind from his granny's spoon.
This ... strange in the mouth of mountain.
It is the food of the hungry.
It is nowhere on earth.

Amelia Earhart said to me —
I was hacking back a hawthorn hedge
in our field in Ballyarnet
when it spluttered and settled
like an unmanned threshing machine.
She rose from the cockpit, pale and tense,
peeling away a leather helmet,
shaking out her curly hair.
She said to me — her long trousered legs
spindly as a boy, her hands skinny as a pianist,
she looked at me, eye to eye, and said —
my snappers on my shoulder, cap on head,
she shouted, jumping into glarry mud,
Amelia Earhart said to me,
'Put out your cigarette'.

Remembering Bridget Cleary
for Adrienne Maher

At mystery of moonless night
a white horse shivering its skin between her knees.

Through shuttered window, locked door,
they listened – tortured pleas between gargled screams.
John Dunne, his mountainy herbal medicine,
forcing the metallic spoon between her adamant teeth,
clapping his big-boned hand across her mouth
'til scare in her eyes of smothering
brought stillness. Men trapping her feet,
shrieks of *bitch* from the man she married,
imprint of hot poker on her forehead part concealed
by soot.

The first time they held her on the grate
– shallow-breathing of watchers
waiting for the djinn to leave her –
her shouting, *Would you scorch me like a herring?*

No sullen smoulder of late-night turf
when she was laid to burn, belly down,
her perfect human head fogged in agony.

She's gone with the evil back to her own
as they frantically dug drenched peat,
her slung body displacing chill brown bog-water.

Breaking, bruising, burning in her:
free bareback woman
out-cantering fearsome night.

COMING BACK
for Irene

I see my brother
tending a border
of pink nerine
with earth on his hands

on the shoreline
in a fawn woollen hat
and sunglasses
arguing with a woman

at a concert
seated in front of me
looking forward
his mind elsewhere

eating a salad sandwich
on top of Slieve Donard
cloud over Annalong

in a tweed cloth cap
wiping the paws of a white dog
with a dark blue towel

he inhabits
my unsuspecting
and better than
hospital machines
the end of his broken
unfinished self.

THE UNBEARABLE UNTIDINESS OF LIVING
for my ninety-seven-year-old aunt, Gertrude

Where did this cardigan come from?

Were you out at the house?

Who left that there?

Will they be letting me home soon?

Wasn't my sister called Carrie?

Don't Leave Me near Maureen Ford's House

The glint of polished silver in the front room:
my eye evasive as an animal's.
Big tub of fertilised orange begonias
at the dull green door,
the lips of its letterbox sealed.

I saw you, older than your mother,
choosing beige and fawn clothes
and once, in worn slippers, sweeping leaves;
on your knees, scrubbing the pavement.

Could it have been us
smirking in the English class
because you said Miss Gilchrist's earrings
looked like warts?

Maureen Ford
you wouldn't even
recognise me.

THE HOUSE ON THE FONTANKA
for Noelle Vial

The taxi driver, dour, pale,
eyes indifferent as St Petersburg sky,
a naked pin-up on his dashboard,
does not know of Anna Akhmatova
or where she lived, panics his car
on the Nevsky Prospekt – wants us
to disembark without a word.

His passenger proclaims, *This is not it.*
This will not do. My friend
cannot walk. Like a long-forgotten dirge
he drones the sounds with resignation,
My friend cannot walk.
My friend cannot walk.

Dancing According to Mr. Khrushchev
for Leland Bardwell

Or take these new dances ...
some of them are completely improper.
You wiggle a certain part of the
anatomy, if you'll pardon the expression.
It's indecent. As Kogan once said to me
when she was looking at the fox-trot,
I've been married twenty years
and never knew this kind of activity
is called the fox-trot.

with violet nail varnish
and her hair dyed with henna;
a smile into my eyes saying
Colour your toenails like rainbows;
redden your hair to the setting sun.
Ink in butterflies on your ankles,
words of love on your wrists.
Fill your teeth with thick gold
and laugh – because,
lady, you and I,
we have enough of everything
but time.

AT KRASI
for Kate

An ancient plane tree, filigree shadows.
Twelve strong men cannot
surround its girth. Water
colder than snow;
and Irene, meaning peace,
her taverna up in the branches
of almonds and figs and ripening apricots.
Vines springing new green grapes
above our airy heads. Wine from the barrel,
a salad as high as the mountain top we're hugged
    against.
Bread, warm grain smell of the sun,
pale red wine trickling from wood.
A day so poured full to running over
that twelve strong men
couldn't get their arms around it.

NOTES TOWARDS MY OWN RETABLO

I'd have to paint the sun
dying – winter fir trees.
A lorry of animal carcasses
bursting into the car.
My face on stones,
stones in my eyes.
I know I have to say
my child and where.
I speak in bloody tongues.

Santo Nino
maybe it was you
who stopped the metal spear my veins, my heart,
my eyes, my brain.

KATE NEWMANN

Columbus in La Isabella

WHAT COLUMBUS SAW

Mango, papaya, cactus,
yucca, coconut, banana;
sanctuary and succulence,
a place to be.
Saw no one until he had to see
Taino Indians taught in the language of their blood,
thirst of fever sweating his men to ground,
the stain and callous on a Spanish palm
blinding out the life-lines, love-lines.
The broken earth, dust of new graves.
An end to one journey,
a beginning of himself despite
the river dried, the distance to the nearest well.
His colonial eyes viewed the sense
the senselessness
and saw that he'd arrived.

WHAT THE SPANISH BROUGHT

All that sea-borne terror,
manatees in dream,
warm flesh thoughts from the cold,
marinated fantasy;
wine and thirst and terracotta tiles,
ships and wood and impossible distance,
men and men and men and hunger,
swords of solid sunlight,
prayer and paleness,
phlegm and fever and dry fear,
dying and living and dying.

TAINO INDIAN WORDS

Who named the Taino, Taino?
The broad span of the skull,
their shaven heads like new-born.

Coca.
The green of lost innocence
and how they shared it from a ritual tray.

Tobacco.
The deepest brown, brown of river-bed,
brown of skin parched under this sun,
inhaling their capacity to live.

Papaya.
Teeth embedded in the fleshiest fruit,
the hungriest juice, this place.

And when the smell of pitch and urine,
of salt-drunk wood, had left the nostrils,
Canoe.
The silence of a colluding tree
escaping through sunlit blues.

Oh coca, tobacco, papaya, canoe.

The words, the words –
the least they took.

The House of Christopher Columbus

It is still a good place to be
the house of Christopher Columbus.
Built like a church, open to the quiet bay,
his hearth an altar.
A house to forget in
as heat paled the palms,
sea lisped forgiveness,
all the doors for escape.
A house to let the man believe,
drink fine wine, poor water
and know the worth of being alive.

BLOOD IN THE TREES

Flamboyan, flamboyan,
flame flowers held at arm's length,
flame in sunlight, blood-red.

Trees greener than lust for home,
flourishing while they wasted, fevered away.

Water enough, blood enough for these trees,
their flowers fresh gashes in the bluest sky.

Something familiar about this most alien space.
We all know the taste of our own blood.

YUCCA

Not the smoky oregano of mountain lamb
wrapped in straw, baked in a clay pot,
coarse salted, washed down
with last year's wine.

The meat of this island,
a pappy confusion on the tongue,
filling the mouth with absence,
its bulk in the belly.

Ground to fine flour, a savage bread –
no rising in it.
Food of lovelessness, food of hunger.
A man could fail on a diet of yucca.

First Church in the New World

The foundations, the blood-red soil.
A small rectangle of earth, the first
Church in the New World.
A living tree shedding serenity
with shadow of its leaves
has rooted beneath the stone, coming up
serpentine, reaching for sustenance, for grace
where the altar might have been –
like the hand of God
clutching a fistful of ground,
in a resignation, a capitulation
to the reach of sky,
the claim of clay.

The Spaniard

Cholera, malaria, his anthem of the place.
His arms crossed over his ribs,
a Christian dying.
Chicken wire between him and our gaze.
Air empty of mourning.
The Spanish sailor, long bones loose against stone,
soil settling in the consummate curve of his skull,
ribcage letting slats of light,
eye-sockets dark with history,
teeth still spitting the foetid foreign air.

The Dead Dog

That is Christopher Columbus' dog.
A burial casket dug up by archaeologists
left stranded on the porch,
an oval of hard clay,
a murmur of bones, of decay,
and that is Christopher Columbus' dog.
Did he get his share of ship's rations?
Did he cower in the galley through the worst of
  storm?
Oh, Christopher Columbus found a place –
his house – his dog – his colonial heart
opening to heat and light –
a disaster.

WHITE CROSSES

White crosses – when death doesn't ask your name.
White crosses – random markers of the rotting
    embrace between flesh and soil.
White crosses – knowing that wherever we walk, we
    walk on graves.
Goose-bumps, rumours in the heat,
the spitting tremor of a spirit in our spine.
There among the flaming flamboyan,
the skin-pink grasses, cactus wall,
so far from old old worlds,
white crosses,
ghosts of misery, ankle-high.

LEAVING FOR SPAIN

He'd have to leave the dog.
A ship with tobacco, cocoa, salt fish,
maize bread, dried mango,
amber, silver, larimar, gold
to hold between him and the burning shame.
Forgotten, the shape
of all he'd once loved,
trying to map in it
an outline of Spain.
How to navigate against the current
of his living desire?
He prayed alone, one taper lit,
kneeling to his New World God,
his own.

CHRISTOPHER COLUMBUS RETURNS
TO LA ISABELLA

It castrates a man
to be where he is not.
And two years almost too long
in limbo to fight your way
back into heaven, onto earth.
All that time, while he had
drowned in Spain's best wine
and glutted on the food of night,
he'd been looking back through eyes
at the sun on this sea,
dreaming manatee.

It finishes a man
to find that where he is, is not;
to find a dereliction of the heart.
Fire dead in the hearth,
cactus trees gesticulating insult
where they'd been tamed.
He cried, a eunuch to his own emotions,
cuckolded by the adultery of place.

The Roof Tiles

Stacked in neat piles as though
waiting for Christopher Columbus
to return to the once-new world
and mend his roof.
Terracotta tiles, their hand-made contours,
each casting an arc of shadow
as though they know what the others
   are thinking:
of paella and fingers against guitar strings in the night;
of white pigeons and the rolling
Andalusian accent of the clouds;
of dust and siesta and the surviving rhythms
of an old man asleep;
of women at the birth;
of Holy Water sprinkled at the wake.

Not this savage sun,
this ruthless soil,
this easy, uneasy dying,
this pitiless, pitiless rain.

BULULA'S CAFÉ

At Bulula's Café you can have
a large bottle of cold beer,
pork slow-cooked over a low wood fire
with onion and spices and beans
inside the lean-to kitchen.
Glutinous rice and peppers and sparse pale salad
and yellow yucca like sweet play-dough
and Bulula's grand-daughters will offer you more,
her great grand-sons watching and
sugar cane as far as the eye can.
Green shadows, and shadows under the eyes
of Bulula's daughters, daughters-in-law,
smiling, enduring, surviving each other
and the heat in the tin-roofed, three-roomed house.
And when you ask the address,
Bulula's son will write:
Mariel
Bulula
Enma
Zulica
Aleja
Jose
Juana
Indira
Angel
Andrea
Berto
Beronica
Chico
Mecho
Telefono 1.223.0783
and you'll never feel so welcome,
so unrelated.

THE VAN AT BULULA'S

has pale pink plastic dishes,
aluminium pans, mops, cheap cutlery,
detergent, tin-openers, soap.

Bulula's daughter with her hair in rollers
bantering with the driver;
Bulula scrutinizing unimpressed.

The van at Bulula's, with toothpaste
and tumblers, flip-flops and T-towels,
gossip about Rio Grande.

The man of the van at Bulula's
knows if he stays here long enough
we'll all find what it is we've been looking for.

Zoo

Iguanas
prefer sweet-cake from tourists
to their natural diet.
These iguanas in a tin nightmare,
heat pounding on metal,
pounding on reptilian skin.
All mistreated membrane.

Tourists draped with curl of snake,
sellotaped *To stop it toilet.*
Hung on our bodies
a necklace of pain.

Musk of huge feathers
falling to the floor.
Cage narrower than wing-span,
remembered eucalyptus,
mangroves, flight.
Failing flesh staring staring.
We'd never seen
wish we'd never seen there
Golden Eagle.

In cruelest daylight
owl chicks, minah birds.
The mother owl
a hunch of fury, of disbelief.

The eyes.
The eyes wired in.

GOAT SKETCH

No need to sketch the sinister buzz,
that black excitement of carrion flies,

nor the heavy inhalation
of life rotting into day.

No need to draw the unsurfaced mountain road,
myrtle, thyme, sun-stained grasses.

Only the anatomy of goat,
a stomach bloat brown,

the bladder dead to light,
an udder leaning into dust.

Hooves in disarray – a mad escape
in all directions in this icon of ending.

The head – colour of cinnamon on rice pudding –
the severed head: a gentle John the Baptist lying on
clay.

Soft nostrils of breathed-out fear, lips holding quiet
their memory of carob nibbled from high branches.

White whiskers – and the eyes
wide open blue to our unseeing.

FLYING FISH
for Yannis

Through the raucous light
I've seen them fly – wild flicker
across belief, longer than possible,
as long as you can hold your breath.

Fish when it breaches the water
– sudden, featherless, a gasp –
it swims through day, its pectoral fins frantic,
its cold blood furious with joy.

A bolt from the glugging gutterals of ocean
into the hollow song of air;
that flight from who we are,
never knowing the shadow we cast.

Believing in the stretch of water,
the dream to dive through,
it is gone again into fish,
abandoning us to question:

Does it ever fear its own absence?
Does it ever fear to drown
in the depth of sky?

THE CHARCOAL BURNERS OF MELIDONI, CRETE

Their days porous and smudged,
the charcoal burners never leave
the piles of ancient olive wood
stacked in ritual mounds.

Sculptors of the untouched,
the unseen, their eyes stare
as though the smothered burning happens
in their skulls. They read the sweet reek

of smoke, ease air holes through ash,
careful as singers controlling their breathing.
And you can't stay long
near their smoke-blackened skins

in that carbonised silence,
and you won't be there
when they finish this liturgy of charring;
when they solemnly uncover

charcoal – all the shape of aftermath,
like everything you're not allowed to say
come back to light
for a second chance at burning.

EL GRECO
for Ted Deppe

*Fodhele in Crete is reputedly where Domenikos Theotokopoulos,
known as El Greco, was born in 1541*

i

He never went back
but carried in his head
the sharp cicada shrill,
the anatomy of home.

ii

In Venice – Titian's studio.
Amid the promiscuous
mingling of pigments,
he held behind his eyes
the flat guilt, the quiet
of the monks in Crete
leaning towards Byzantium,
the exact tilt of the Virgin's head.

iii

In Rome, with his mother's tight-lipped
disapproval, he threw back his head
to dismiss Michaelangelo's nudes
though he envied the Italian
his adoration of the flesh,
began feverishly modelling
his own figures from wax
before lifting a brush.

iv

In Toledo he caught the shadows
on the skin cast by the Inquisition.
When the priests refused
his *Disrobing of Christ*
– the beautiful forearm
of the carpenter making the cross –
he fought them like a feuding neighbour.

v

He stayed in the cool religious fervour,
spent days in a darkened room
neither working nor sleeping,
but crossing Fodhele river,
following the path through orange and lime groves,
wild thyme and Jerusalem sage.

vi

He painted limbs like flames;
eyes harrowed with piety;
bodies moon-blanched, asymmetrical;
robes the furious greens of Cretan maple
in noon-day sun, the livid, lurid pinks
of crushed mulberries; skies heavy
with the charcoal clouds that gather
over Mount Ida.

vii

The King of Spain hated his vision,
strident with acid reminders
of elsewhere and other.

viii

He hired twenty-four rooms
with gardens, orange trees, lime trees,
a private orchestra to drown out
the rasping lust of cicada song
in the deepest heat.

ix

His turbulent fingers mastered
the art of painting sanctity,
exquisite serenity in the bones of the hand.

x

He never came back, The Greek, El Greco,
his son a Spaniard, his woman unmarried.
He died in obscurity, The Greek,
El Greco, in Spain - dark heresy
staring from the pupils of his Cretan eyes.

xi

What he left behind: seventy-two books –
little other property.

In Père-Lachaise Cemetery, Paris

Why did we choose to come here –
this crowded arrondissement of the dead
breathing with the soil?

We drank dark Cahors from the bottle,
our voices thick in the mossed acoustic,
our heavy flesh displacing light.

The dead accommodated each other like old
    neighbours.
We were strangers, blackening the air
like winter acacias aching for lost yellow.

We walked their hushed streets,
lichen peeling like distemper,
the dead waiting for us to leave,

dull to our silent revelation
that we had lost each other
back before we met.

MAGENTA BOULEVARD
for Maggie

The market gives back to the street
a picture of being French
painted in boucherie vermilions:
alizarin crimsons of lamb;
pork a permanent rose;
horsemeat, Camargue sunset,
cadmium reds dense with escape.

In the fromagerie, camembert
bulges ripe perfection
from a rind of yellow ochre.

Sap green bottles, nudged
precariously on a narrow shelf,
promise to flood our gentle world
with scarlet lake, rose madder.

By leaded glass, pthalo blue,
fingered tarot cards.
Framed certificates in sepia
spell out the dates
when Claude and Bernard Lalire
were born, confirmed, accepted
into The Order
of St.Genevieve,
four years apart.

On Magenta Boulevard
women in Payne's grey,
Gamboge and Hooker's green,
burnt siennas, raw umbers,
finger through the worn-out dyes

of a second-hand clothes stall.
As lamp black washes over ivory black,
our soles our palms our eyes
chill with Chinese white.

SACRÉ COEUR

The full moon a huge flatbread
mopping up the spiced Montmartre dark.
We climb the acutes and graves
over the smoulder of late city.
We lean out over the balcony of night
above the perilous slant of cobbled streets,
where the gloved elderly couple
sell apricots and blue cheese,
water costlier than wine;
wait to go home to their shuttered dreams.

The Sacré Coeur, a vast body of stone
forgives us our blood,
our warm complicity with the rubble of memory.
While silent pigeons cradle from cold
Sacré Coeur translates the profanity
of our greedy prayers,
forgives us our flesh,
our blameless skin.

HOTEL KYRIAD, PARIS

Wakened by torrential rain,
I lie inside your breath,
remember a campsite in Bois du Bologne,
an afternoon tented with ambivalent grey,
my mother in dark blue, and me
in the damp collusive cavern,
its mildew consolation,
the raw silence of her crying
beating louder on the eardrum of memory
than the rain, the rain persistent as my watching.

Years later I found French Linguaphone notes
in my father's scrawl – the tutor's comment
Don't try to be so ambitious in what you express.

You haven't stirred. The light on Rue Letort
has wasted while we slept.

A wedding party in Elfichaoui Salon du Thé
sweats heady crescendo onto the street,
its flourescent bulbs flickering.

When did my father stop trying?
Why, on that family holiday
when I was six
can I only count two of us
on the abacus of love?

Before We Know Who We Are

We come into this world
like warm vowels
in the mouth,

already sensing the echo
of pigeon song from the soft ruins
of the future,

swoon of hawthorn blossom
in dark rain breathing
into fecund night.

Our leveret limbs push against air
with the hare's fine-boned
thrust on earth.

When my mother learned
that she carried me, she walked
five miles in deep snow,

became the sunset
that never set,
so that I was born tasting dusk,

holding under my skin
all imaginary flight-paths
to hover me above harm.

BIRD IN THE HAND
in memory of James Simmons

There was cold and amber
and gold leaf dulling in the sky.
Roubles too much and not enough
for the currency of the day.
We bought you a balsa bird, as light as
the cotton thread from which it hung.

A single piece of wood
the man explained,
his hands turning the foreign words
to show fragility,
a body without a break, without a join,
smelling of pencil shavings,
grained like the neck of a well-worn guitar.

The bird's wings thinner than feathers,
too light to hold in the hand
like the palpable terror of the bird
stunning us all as it stunned itself
against the window before
recovering the air.

Too light to hold palpitating in the hand
the memory of you at the end,
taking a bird-like morsel
of grilled mackerel;
a hover of charcoal blue distance,
wood-smoke lingering in my hair.

MAYO TRAINS

The steaming sorrow
of the first train
as it lurched to Achill Sound;
a parched barque for the bodies
of drowned men taken from the sea.
What was it drew them, made them bolt
sudden to the edge of the hooker,
its tarred belly bloat against the waves,
its sails slapping a black cautious morse?
What was it there that drew them
jolt together to pound against the spliced ribs
into the sudden parabola
of their boast future,
the hooker floating in the calm
like a drowned man's black shoe?

And the last train from Westport
gulping back its sad fumes through Kilmeena's
over-ripe blackberries and coming rain,
bringing to one family
two brothers of the eleven
tattie hokers
burned in a Scottish hut
kept locked at night.
The stone weight of the men,
the breathlessness of the carriage's pulse,
the throbbing memory of clay,
the hideous music of poverty and death
poverty and death
on the baffle of sleepers.

St Vincente Tagua Tagua, Chile

Catching in its name the gutteral cry
of migrating geese – Tagua Tagua.
Settled under memories of subsistence and snow
and the moon-cold nights of the mountains.

In the market, buckets of seaweed,
glaucous strips to bulk out meatless stew.
Ravenous heat of noon and hands
weighing hefty tomatoes and wild wilting spinach,

mauve heads of garlic and fresh onions
and everywhere a superstitious dust.
Shelled walnuts and cumin,
olives as black as knowing eyes.

At the same stall each week, a man
whose hens once laid double-yoked eggs
sees through the albumin of our alien words
to the cracked-shell outline of the Andes.

THE WIDOW'S CANTINA, ST VINCENTE
TAGUA TAGUA, CHILE

No place for pity among the bottles and the sleepless
dust.
Unopened cherry brandy
paling to liverish on the high shelf;
aguardienthe, sugar, pisco sour,
spilt syrupy talk of other women's husbands.
Morning wine bottles with their vinegar breath
on her reputation.

No place for pity in the house
of stone floors and Jesus.
Potato peelings curling from her widowed hands
like fleshy divinations of survival.
The air in the good room pinioned in the past
with photographs of her seven children.

Cut trees sprouting by the sawmill,
rats eating the base of her clay oven.
No place for pity among the coralled pigs,
all hide and suckling beside the hen run,
snouts snuffling out her omniverous loneliness,

a hollow in the fire-pit
where flame would follow slaughter
and neighbours come as the night
rendered all of them down
to leg and loin and belly,
knuckle end, shank, spare rib;
those hopelessly familiar bones.

A Night in St Vincente Tagua Tagua, Chile

The musky night pressing into its memory
peach-skin and apricot, the mutinous bulk
of a pumpkin clinging to the ground.

We are gentle mutterings on the soft palate of earth,
wrapped in oldest slumber, our bodies
moulded from adobe dreams.

When time coughs, we sense it through the quiet
of a pale blue door with dimpled glass,
but need not stir.

Salamander-soft, sleep falls like lees
settling in a gourd of silence.
We are like listening honey.

Mrs Carrute, St Vincente Tagua Tagua, Chile

Seventeen years since her husband left.
Under the slur of sky
her house aches with decorum,
her flesh expanding inside its rind of shame.

Night-dew on the sucked pink of cultivated roses,
on the lascivious red of wild poppies
scattering themselves among the anchorage
of her golden gladioli, stiff hollyhocks.

She swallows the surge of colour,
the wine a distillation of broken vows
dilating the arteries of dark with oblivion,
her tongue slippery with smuggled sounds.

She sees a straggle of couch grass and nettle
through the tended stalks, bees honing the air to a
      hunger
louder than gossip. His shape
between them like a ghostly succulent.

Tomorrow she will stake out the ambivalent day
quietly, find absolution in the soft lap
of agave syrup pancakes, geranium cuttings
stemming the rumour with their innocent anodyne.

SANTA RITA VINEYARD, CHILE

Above the cellars, Saint Rita's statue,
her velvet dress the colour of old wine,
its pile worn down by desperate fingers.
Patron Saint of midwives,
Patron Saint of hopeless cases.

In the vineyard, the earth, a vellum of sin.
Sun pounding remorseless,
the mountains loud with the flat acoustic
of intoxicating heat.

Vines and light trained in immaculate rows
kept alive by the melt-water of our fears
running down from the Andes
cloudy with rock-flour.

Red roses – damascus, cerise –
deciphering the hot air
for fungus and decay.

The grapes
leguminous gestations
in the amniotic silence.

Saint Rita,
Patron Saint of hopeless cases,
Patron Saint of midwives,
knowing all there is to know
about bodies,
about blood.

THE WIVES OF PABLO NERUDA

Maria Antonieta Hagenaar

How did we invent
that mutating vocabulary
of chromosomes and blame?

Her, carrying in her lowland genes
all that eye-level water,
that old-world sin.

Foreignness and fear
filling the cavity in their daughter's brain,
distending her perfect supple skull.

Hydrocephalus – its ancient language of guilt,
smells of birth and pity, death and pity.
She was the end of their beautiful lineage,

his only defeating poem of paternity
swaddled in mute black ink. He wore her
profile in his eyes, a cameo of sterile love.

Lost to each other and forever bound.
A knotted chord, a matrimonial of spermatozoon with
    ovum,
marking their anniversaries

on a new calendar of eight-year spans.
Their eyes cast down.
Their foreheads bursting with grief.

Delia del Carril

Her paintings exposed in black and white
the sinew and bone of betrayal
beneath all our skins.

What he loved her for –
those twenty years
leaning before him.
A canvas free of children,
free of stretch marks;
a canvas as broad as the Andes,
the murmur of ice from Argentina
scintillating his unmarked borders.

Hormiguita he called her
– little ant – but she didn't mind
as she scurried behind her eyes
with all his time,
her desires an army marching
back under the pallet of her skin
with his beauty, piece by piece.

Matilde Urrutia

Lost in his conceits
of laurels and onions and laughing pianos,
his voyage through the autumn of her hair,

she emerges in the sad precision of a champagne
    cocktail,
in the impeccable red wing-span of an embalmed
cola-cola bird flown, encased, from Venezuela.

Faded perfumes,
an empty mirror,
the gentile hunger of forgotten dresses.

Bird-like clip, clip, clip of her turquoise satin stilettos
as a slow waltz is shadowed on the antique tiled floor,
a silk garden in the folds of her kimono.

Huddled at the foot
of Cerro San Cristobal Zoo,
camel-pulse and tiger-breath
heaving a diction of defeat;
the sultry side-winding,
belly-scale creeping of snakes,
their mating body loops.

In the red-wine cool interior
a row of Russian dolls,
inside each, another vowel-empty carcass.
On his desk the astrolabe
telling of constellations – Hydrus,
Leo, Lupus, Camelopardus –
captive in the stale skies
of the imagination.

Cigarette smoke ensnared in the red pile of velvet
    curtains,
faded hospitality and the matted phrases
of scandalous memory.

The bedroom is forbidden, its wild-cat pull
into the blind tumble of desiring limbs,
the private joke of hormones and need
grating on the nerves of heat,
the phonetics of sleep and rattling phlegm.

Neruda sensed his hopeless oscillation
in the unrelenting evolution of species,
sloughed his thoughts

into the discarded skin of poetry,
smelling the danger of terrible captivity,
smelling the danger of terrible release.

LA SEBASTIANA
PABLO NERUDA'S HOUSE IN VALPARAISO

From here the Pacific becomes a map of abstraction,
etching the unthinkable past, too wide for words.

A narrow dance of corridor and cramp;
crows-nest dreams of foraging in soil.

Above the livid heat it craves the rank slap
of waves in the working port.

Built to take in all of Valparaiso,
La Sebastiana desires the flight of passerine thoughts,

their startling white and silver escape
against hot unwitting Valparaiso blues

like pigeons disappearing, like fragments
of misremembered songs.

It is all too late, too overworked:
the cumbersome armchair nicknamed *la nube* (the
cloud);

the footstool stained with green ink;
the fingered patina of type-writer keys

and a wind-up gramophone mixing meaninglessly
with voices from beneath the insufferable window –

its undiscerning glass an impossible page
for amphibious nightmares and free-falling verse.

Crammed with frigates and schooners –
ships becalmed in bottles
by the rope-rough hands
of a seaman from Coronel.

As though the house is dry-docked
by Neruda's love, his fear, of the sea –
Venus riding a sea-horse,
a black mermaid from Venice, beached
among the furniture.

Figureheads lean towards the lodestar
of his terror, resignation weighing
in their wooden breasts,
their sad porcelain eyes condensing oceans,
mourning those poems never embarked upon.

THE ENTRANCE HALL OF ISLA NEGRA
for Shay O'Byrne

A crude spiral of sea-shells
embedded in the circular floor.

Neruda asked that guests enter barefoot,
so that before sipping his singular cocktail,

donning a beret or panama
from the walk-in wardrobe,

(ponchos hanging self-consciously
beside his Nobel tuxedo, worn once),

before enduring the land-locked chatter
under the mural of lapis, onyx and quartz,

he would have them remember, heel, arch, callous,
the nakedness of skin.

PABLO NERUDA'S STUDY AT ISLA NEGRA

A refuge from the gatherings,
Covatcha – his favourite study.

A stove, too beautiful a black iron belly
to need lit.

Matilde's sombre portrait.
The dull ecclesiastical weight of a brass hand.

Covatcha – rain pounding
its metrical death on the zinc roof.

A stuffed jay beyond silence.
Wood, breathing elipses and line-breaks,

the grain of living honed to a morticed quiet.
And the flotsam desk that lurched towards him

from the agonised sea
wordless and worn,

waiting to feel waves of genius break,
gasping out from the undertow of language.

PABLO NERUDA'S GLOBE

A papier-mâché sphere stretched
round the diurnal emptiness of death,
it darkens the room on its huge axis.

They could not understand when he brought
this nineteenth-century world from England,
crossing with it lines of longitude and latitude.

He was amused when the customs officials
cut open the ocean, expecting to hold gravity
in their prosaic hands.

Caught in the magnetic pull of consonant to vowel,
Pablo Neruda desired to clutch to him
the unfathomable universe.

THE HORSE PARLOUR

The colossal painted horse of his childhood,
salvaged from the saddlery in Temuco,
scavenged across forty-five years.

Reminding him of salted corn, steaming in the hand,
its plaster joints, its dolls' eyes
ready for any journey back to himself

– Ricardo Eliecer Neftali Reyes Basalto –
his father coming in, dark with engine oil
and fatigue.

The once unattainable horse surrounded with real hay
in the house loud with childlessness
which only knew him old,

its gloss brown flanks, cream fetlocks
silently stabled: Neruda's furthest past
tethered to what never was.

PABLO NERUDA'S PRIVATE ROOM

A cubicle of Victorian pornography
the bathroom, meant only for his menfriends.

Sturdy women in copious corsets;
layers of flounced petticoat;
sepia breasts, broad aureoles;
eyes fixed on the camera;
bare skin and buttoned boots;
pubic hair and loose-laced bodices;
fingers poised against pubes,
held for the slow prurience of shutter-speed.

The red devil on the door
grimaces wearily into flaccid air
at the stale choreography of sin.

The door of the kitchen
remains titillatingly shut.
Neruda wrote across it:
Don't look at what doesn't matter to you.

PABLO NERUDA'S STORE ROOM

Gathering to him the rarified words,
collecting the objects and their names.

A cowrie-shell nestling in the writing hand,
primordial, seductive, vocal as absence.

The conch – that ultimate storm blast
pounding the abdomen into the depth of unsaid.

Giant clams from the Philippines,
lips curled around an empty guttural.

Haunted by nomenclatures,
he sought out the endangered

monodon monoceros –
sea unicorn – *narwhale*,

procuring its legendary tusk
with the money from his Nobel Prize.

Pablo Neruda's store room
ripe with unopened boxes,

a borrowed dictionary of ocean
lusting into language.

PABLO NERUDA'S HUT

He edged down the rough path
where climbing geraniums

kept their succulent hold
on the afternoon.

Wind's crazy iambs shunting
past the warp of wooden slates.

Surreptitious genius of spiders and weevils,
the sensuous lure of neglect.

Driven by half-heard phrases
punctuated by the lamp's splutter

he hid from the invasive sky
and the dull anchor of conversation,

allowed the fugitive dark
to lie uninhibited on the dusty page.

PABLO NERUDA'S BEDROOM

It was from here
he saw through a brass telescope
the desk-top floating towards him.

His bedroom where night peers through empty bottles
and sleep drinks the poetry
of dead friends.

His bed nailed to the floor
ready for storm,
tacking into the current,

its coverlet a white
foaming filigree
of his sister's crocheted love.

Lamp oil and night-shuffle,
surgical stockings, the broken
sentence of reticent urine burning.

WATER IS BETTER DRUNK
FROM COLOURED GLASS

In all Pablo Neruda's houses
coloured glass startling the air
out of its complacency.

Discordant dreams refracting the word,
warping the flat world into a ghostly oasis.

> Water is better drunk
> from coloured glass.

Rust of red-wine nights
and obsidian friendship,
chandeliers and shatter.

Greens of cactus
and fishing floats.
and unripe figs.

A dark woman
over the Blue Curacao Pacific
raising to her lips a glass of ocean.

> Water is better drunk
> from coloured glass.

Two hundred and eighty-six bottles
empty with the stale air of French markets,
naked between the meniscus of blank-staring
windows.

Turquoise recycled from Tequila memories,
the glass-blower's breath
still haunting the nose with hard-won wisdom and
cheap cigarettes.

            Water is better drunk
            from coloured glass.

The hungry neck of a bottle
in the fluted lips of the wind
like a dulcimer of death

sings of time's erosion
at the frantic shore of us
wearing us to sand.

            Water is better drunk
            from coloured glass.

Fusing anew to a pristine echo,
a bloodless afterlife,
neither liquid nor solid nor language.

Renewable as moon.
Transparent as love, as breakable.

            Water is better drunk
            from coloured glass.

All along we drank only
from the inadequate chalice of each other
and ourselves.

A sanctuary in the gouty quiet,
forgetting the bodies that had fallen farther than
    foreboding.
A pisco sour glistening in a sugared glass –
the ice-fires of Patagonia.

At home with cement dust from labourers' boots,
the inky cling of newspaper print to skin,
the slow drip of a faulty tap
marking a rusty stain in the pocked enamel basin.

The bottles of good vintage
dark-ageing, histories away
from the distant beauty of Atacama,
llamas nibbling the expansive light.

The elderly barman
– older than Neruda when he died –
wearing a waistcoat too large,
walking a stone floor worn free of metaphor.

THE DAY OF THE VIRGIN,
CERRO SAN CRISTOBAL, SANTIAGO

Feet drawn up the silent mountain
by something older than the notion of sin.

Flatbreads tarnished with woodsmoke
and lost sleep, wrapped in the city's news.

Eggs hard-boiled by strangers,
each a peeled and saltless promise in the hand.

A llama in a woven robe, pigeons and bunched
    peonies,
icons polished by the heat.

Amber lilies, armfuls of dizzying yellows,
carried into the unappeasable eye of sun.

The sun-deep flow of urine
as a child squats in the ditch.

Absolving us into aloneness
the day becomes a vast prayer.

THE DESCENT FROM CERRO SAN CRISTOBAL

Gone the elderly couple with stigmata
stained on their hands;

gone the family pulling a push-chair
with a broken wheel;

gone the father with his daughter on his shoulders,
her feet beneath his armpits, holding on;

Everyone is parched penance,
drawn to the illicit relief of a water sprinkler.

They gather the papery flicker
of wild corn from the hill –

husks of light to see them through
the unholy days ahead.

LOTA, CHILE, AFTER THE
COAL MINES CLOSED
for Megan

Lota is a weary man sitting on his step.
It is the sea bartering salt memories with the shore.
It is a solitary trumpeter practising

in the porch of a derelict theatre,
the music amazed by the acoustic
of a whole sky.

Lota is the weight of coal-dust in the pores.
It is aguardiente sipped in an open doorway;
sea-gull cries and salt-fish.

Lota is a white hospital above the park
of limetrees and almonds and marble statues.
It is the aftertaste of privilege.

Lota is red lipstick, an old woman in stilettoes
staring at a Fortune Machine;
a carton of good cheap wine.

Lota is a barrow of fresh boiled crabs;
stalls of umbrellas and dusty figs;
the ooze through brown paper of home-made cheese.

Lota is a cathedral of late-afternoon.
It is already half way home to oregano and onions
over a low flame.

Lota is a seamstress hemming a gaberdene coat.
It is a dress of green seduction;
hands reaching for today's hot bread.

Lota is strange as the stare of fishes' eyes.
It is a tethered dog.
The earth naked as an old lie.

Lota is a communist mural on a peeling gable.
A sulky hammering in the scrapyard.
It is nowhere near the Andes.

Lota is the church loud with the curdled silence
of an empty mine.
Thoughts clog the lung of prayer.

Lota is the tired shoulders of a working man,
the smudge of his rolled-up newspaper,
his laboured breath.

Lota is a graveyard gleaming white headstones
on a distant hill. Cried-out years and fossilized anger.
Bones of miners going back.

VIRGIN DEL CARBON

The Virgin, hewn from the coal-face,
brought up to the light.
How we chisel from our fear
the anatomy of our devotion.

She comes from a place
beyond fecundity, deeper than decay,
dimmer than the bass note
of ocean's moan.

She watches over men
who mine echoes,
offering up a weariness of limbs,
a faith in ascension:

men who know the immaculate hold
that sterile black dust
has on the lining of their lungs,
colonising each dark shaft of breath.

Before the miracle with the fireman,
the levitations and the visions;
before the fever burned her up
when she was nineteen,
she is a pale icon,
chin perfecting the tilt between
self-possession and self-denial.
For is it not heaven
on earth to live with God?

She falls into the smoky sepia of a novice
reluctant to eye the camera.
Her Conscience Diary crucified each day
into twenty-four obstinate squares,
unforgiving hour by unforgiving hour,
symmetrical as her colonial town
trapped beneath its hypotenuse of heat.

On entering the Convent
she hacked her magnificent hair,
buried her long body in brown.
For when I have nothing
then I have least desire.

In the family portrait
loud with clocks and camphor,
a heavy canopy of damask and brocade.
She leans towards her mother,
smells the musty expectations exuding from her skin.

At six years, poised on the steps
in a double-breasted winter coat,
she knows she is a saint.

At two years old they have her
ugly in a satin dress, already
making herself hard to love.

No mystery to her the indoctrination of light
through a narrow school window, its frame rotting.

Lucila Godoy Alcayaga from the Elqui Valley
took the pennames *Alguien, Soledad, Alma,*

then became Miss Mistral, marshalling her hours
into hemlines and chalk and restless feet,

blazers and Shakespeare,
a door left banging down a corridor emptied of
    children,

the moon echoing in the depth
of the classroom's dogmatic throat.

Toasting Gabriela Mistral in Il Circulo Italian Restaurant, Chile

Sobranies and beer furtive in the once-college
not-quite restaurant.

A teacher here for six years, Gabriela Mistral
slid her thoughts into sensible button shoes;

heard the scansion of their spinster echo
rendered on waxed walnut;

was glad to be hexagoned in the honeycomb of fatigue
inside the geometry of bent heads,

safe from the angry wine of elsewhere,
the crazy unpredictable lyrics of thin mountain air.

Poetry itself was a savage regime
holding her by the nape of her fear,

rescuing her from colourless rigidity,
rescuing her from drowning in her feral dreams.

THE MAN WHO DID NOT WIN THE NOBEL PRIZE FOR LITERATURE

It was all ochre-fade and defeat.
The deluding cat-tongue comfort
of the rough page, each letter
curling in on its utterance.

Ink in his eyes, the books breathing disappointment.
His library an alphabet of betrayal
from Aristotle to Zamyatin
with their backs turned to his self-doubt.

Even the woman on the Botticelli postcard
marking page two-hundred-and-fifteen
of Neruda's *Canto General*
regarded him with distant derision.

Shakespeare Donoso he once signed himself
before he heard his name – $D - o - n - o - s - o -$
as a death knell, a syllabic chant
denouncing him, defining his destiny.

He began to hate the naked battery of type-writer
 keys;
the mothy flitter of his own angry ventricles;
the soft-remembering of his grandmother's garden
with its orange thyme and Corsican mint.

Squinting, he cannot tell
what's in the bags
in his freezer –
the sagging grey stew he made,
and didn't want to eat,
nor throw away;
a single bruised kipper
that has worked its way free
to lodge among the ice-marbles
of last year's gooseberries;
the freezer's breath stale
with the ghost of marmalade oranges.

Meat doesn't go off, he insists,
with the same fervour
he claims there is no God,
and points to Scott's Expedition
– the buried supplies they failed to find
were *fine* years later.

And is this what it is?
Why he has legs of lamb
from nine years ago
stashed there?
Like Tutenkhamun, buried
with twenty-one containers of goat's cheese
for the long wait and for the gods.
Or like Scott, will I find him,
finally frozen, his hand stopped in a last line?
And will he already be trekking the white silence
back to his hoard –
offerings to a spiritless afterlife

where emotions don't matter,
where nothing is subject to change,
where you find intact again, everything
you know you've let decay?

THIRTEEN WAYS OF LOOKING AT CELIBACY

1

He gave me a half-used
bottle of perfume
so I would sit on his
knee in the cinema.
It smelt like his mother.

2

He said *girlfriend*
as if he meant
something else

3

When I touched his thigh
O yes, he groaned,
but it was all he
no I
no he and I

4

When he crossed my threshold
he was all reasonable and reach.
When I crossed his
I found him like a jigsaw piece.

5

George would have climbed down that cliff with me.

6

I didn't know you wanted to come!

7

After seasons under a cold frame
his pallid words – *I am attracted to you* came
close to warmth had he not
uttered them with such shame.

8

I knew you'd understand.

9

He had me so couched
in his terms
I could not comprehend myself.

10

Do you not shave your legs?

11

He called gin 'leg-opener'.

12

My wife would love it here.

13

*The next time I see you, I'm
going to lick you all over.*
The next time he saw me,
he'd forgotten.

Waiting by the Polar Bear
in the Ulster Museum

The Innuit called him *almost a man,*
the great lonely roamer.

He could have waited for hours
or days for a seal to surface for air.

In Belfast his blood has cooled,
his pulse slowed beyond music.

He could have snuggled into drifts of white,
snuffling, turned his back on blizzard.

In Belfast his glassy eye is suspicious,
blinded by lack of love, a hibernation of the heart.

He could have rolled in every word for snow
shimmied his belly across fragile ice, all of him
    belonging.

In Belfast, two layers of fur
could not wrap him from the taxidermist's dull
    dreams.

He could have paddled his great furred paws,
pushed his bulk in deepest water.

Beyond the thinness of Belfast days
he could have licked himself free of all these greys.

THE FOOD MARKET IN DOSTOEVSKY
DISTRICT, ST PETERSBURG

Cherries from Samarkand – seven different
colours of blood. Tomatoes from Tashkent –
red deeper than distance.

Vaster than Siberia, wider than the Black Sea,
the harvest of inexplicable plenty
spread precarious on narrow trestle tables.

Conspicuous in the empty aisles,
foreigners to hunger,
we walk the troubled geography of appetite.

Cheeses from the mountains of Belarus.
Venison, rabbit, boar,
smelling flesh and pale.

How must we smell,
our ethnic mysteries staling the air
with our own particular history?

Outside, a woman in thick stockings
tries to sell a single wilting bunch
of flat-leaf parsley.

Where Dostoevsky Lived

A coffin-sized rectangle
of grey street framed by his balcony door –
all the people and poverty
his soul needed to know.
His hat, shiny and jaded by St. Petersburg air
hung hollow against remembered
birds and fronds of faded wallpaper.

The clock-loud study, staying
the execution of each page;
the blank wall he gave more to,
asked more of
than the hushed children
banished beyond the last line;
the stifled metronome
of his wife's frantic accounts.

His image of Christ taken from the Cross –
each sinew and wound a scrutiny of the flesh
resurrected within us.
That picture, our guide said,
if you stare at it long enough,
will make a Christian of an Atheist,
an Atheist of a Christian.

SONG OF DESPAIR

My friend says he's making designs,
looking at the spaces between things,
the shape of what isn't there.

I wake in the night,
cling to the bulk of your absence,
the curve of my neck and shoulder

craving your unguarded breath;
try to make out the cold outlines
of your silence, the moving arc of loss

traced by a bat flying
its basket-weave into
and out of my dark.

Like the whale imagined,
the raw gulp of salty sky
where the wave has broken.

Luminous dust of stars long-dead
collapsing towards what might have been said.
Hopeless in the ferocious space between us,

the displaced truth, the saddened air;
limbs holding echoes of your limbs,
the shape of what isn't there.

ALEXANDRIA OLD TOWN, WASHINGTON DC, FRIDAY 4AM

Where are they now?
The man lying in the doorway
near the wan magnolias
straggling into random bloom
like a school choir
taking an unrehearsed bow?

He seemed so still
in that bleak street
so close to Zero Mile Stone,
watching the squirrel
slink beneath the cars
stopped at the lights.

And the child in the cancer unit
with a patch on one eye
saying *Bye-bye, Bye-bye*
to the nurses, though he was
about to be admitted?

And the boys in the school
who wrote *Black looks like the alley*
and *My name is from my Dad.
I do know my dad ...?*

And you, whose shifting love shuffles
like someone in the next room
turning pages in the night,
loud with trying to be quiet.

Where are the wild geese
who woke me yesterday,
calling to the heart's tundra?

Now that this vast sky
is dropping vast rain
onto the long-suffering Potomac,
onto this historic wooden house,
its damp ghosts wheezing
into my sleeplessness.

NOT A WORD
for Adrian

I

Peter Ustinov released an imaginary bird
from his cupped hands
and three hundred children
followed its flight path
with their eyes.

II

I am walking from the bookshop.
A man pushes past me, urgent,
clutching a pigeon with a gash on its back.
He carries it so tenderly,
but I cannot be sure
he does not mean it harm.

III

The class have written *Pigeon Song*
            sorrow with a sapphire sound,
            calling into our fears, close to us,
and I want them to release
the imaginary bird.

IV

The first time, Aysha is unconvinced,
embarrassed to cup her hands around nothing.
No one watches its flight.
My voice is becoming crow-like.

V

She tries again – throwing air
up into the air.
For a sapphire moment
the children's eyes follow,
until Taj reaches to the ground,
picks up an invisible sling-shot,
takes perfect aim.
No one lifts the wounded bird.

Riding with a Nomad Tangles Your Hair

His skin smelt of tribal dust,
of funduqs and staying alive
by staying on the move.

And I might have stayed with the nomad,
but for loveless sand
blown against my cautious bones;

but for the low tent
pitched like a haggard night
beside the frayed Algerian border;

but for the camel's head in Tozeur
still soft with intelligence,
blooding the white market wall.

And I might have stayed –
Kufic tremors and Aghlabid gutturals,
tooth-enamel worn to tortoise-shell,

a keffiyeh of paling yellow cotton,
mergoums and kilims,
a cumin, plum and tannin ache beneath my feet,

a lurch of quiet in his unflinching gaze
frightening me by how foreign I have always been,
expecting love to cross

– camel trains and caravanserai –
the vast and shifting desolation
of my unsettled dreams.